To Natalie – on her birthday
January 21st, 1921
from
Helen.

JOSEPH PENNELL'S PICTURES OF THE PANAMA CANAL

FIFTH EDITION

Joseph Pennell's Pictures of the Panama Canal

REPRODUCTIONS OF A SERIES OF LITHOGRAPHS MADE BY HIM ON THE ISTHMUS OF PANAMA, JANUARY—MARCH, 1912, TOGETHER WITH IMPRESSIONS AND NOTES BY THE ARTIST

PHILADELPHIA AND LONDON

J. B. LIPPINCOTT COMPANY

1913

PRINTED BY J. B. LIPPINCOTT COMPANY
AT THE WASHINGTON SQUARE PRESS
PHILADELPHIA, U. S. A.

TO

J. B. BISHOP

SECRETARY OF THE ISTHMIAN
CANAL COMMISSION

WHO

MADE IT POSSIBLE
FOR ME TO DRAW
THESE LITHOGRAPHS

AND

WHO WAS ALSO GOOD
ENOUGH TO ACCEDE
TO MY REQUEST AND
READ AND CORRECT
THE PROOFS FOR ME

INTRODUCTION—MY LITHOGRAPHS OF THE PANAMA CANAL

THE idea of going to Panama to make lithographs of the Canal was mine. I suggested it, and the *Century Magazine* and *Illustrated London News* offered to print some of the drawings I might make.

Though I suggested the scheme a couple of years ago, it was not until January, 1912, that I was able to go—and then I was afraid it was too late—afraid the work was finished and that there would be nothing to see, for photographs taken a year or eighteen months before, showed some of the locks built and their gates partly in place.

Still I started, and after nearly three weeks of voyaging found, one January morning, the Isthmus of Panama ahead of the steamer, a mountainous country, showing deep valleys filled with mist, like snow fields, as I have often seen them from Montepulciano looking over Lake Thrasymene, in Italy. Beyond were higher peaks, strange yet familiar, Japanese prints, and as we came into the harbor the near hills and distant mountains were silhouetted with Japanese trees and even the houses were Japanese, and when we at length landed, the town was full of character reminiscent of Spain, yet the local character came out in the Cathedral, the tower of which —a pyramid—was covered with a shimmering, glittering mosaic of pearl oyster shells. The people, not Americans, were primitive, and the children, mostly as in Spain, were not bothered with clothes.

I followed my instinct, which took me at once to the great swamp near the town of Mount Hope, where so many of De Lesseps' plans lie buried. Here are locomotives, dredges, lock-gates, huge bulks of iron, great wheels, nameless, shapeless masses—half under water, half covered with vines—the end of a great work. I came back to Colon by the side of the French Canal, completed and working up to, I believe, Gatun Lock and Dam, and spent the afternoon in the American town, every house Japanese in feeling, French or American in construction, screened with black wire gauze, divided by white wood lines—most decorative—and all shaded by a forest of palms. Through these wandered well-made roads, and on them were walking and driving well-made Americans. There were no mosquitoes, no flies, no smells, none of the usual adjuncts of a tropical town.

At the end of the town was a monument, a nondescript Columbus, facing nowhere, at his feet an Indian; but it seemed to me, if any monument was wanted at Colon, it should be a great light-house or a great statue towering aloft in the harbor, a memorial to the men who, French and American, have made the Canal.

Next day I started across the Continent to Panama, for I learned the Government headquarters were there, and, until I had seen the officials, I did not know if I should be allowed to work or even stay on the Isthmus. But at Gatun I got off the train, determining to do all I could before I was stopped—as I was quite sure I should be. I saw the tops of the locks only a few hundred yards away, and, turning my back on the stunning town piled up on the hillside, walked over to them; from a bridge bearing a sign that all who used it did so at their own risk I looked down into a yawning gulf stretching to right and left, the bottom filled with crowds of tiny men and tiny trains—all in a maze of work; to the right the gulf reached to a lake, to the left to mighty gates which mounted from the bottom to my feet. Overhead, huge iron buckets flew to and fro, great cranes raised or lowered huge masses of material. As I looked, a bell rang, the men dropped their tools, and lines of little figures marched away, or climbed wooden stairs and iron ladders to the surface. The engines whistled, the buckets paused, everything stopped instantly, save that from the depths a long chain came quickly up, and clinging to the end of it, as Cellini would have grouped them, were a dozen men—a living design—the most decorative motive I have ever seen in the Wonder of Work. I could not have imagined it, and in all the time I was on the Isthmus I never saw it but once again. For a second only they were posed, and then the huge crane swung the group to ground and the design fell to pieces as they dropped off.

Across the bridge was a telephone station and beyond and below it the great approaches to the locks along which electric locomotives will draw the ships that pass through. There was a subject, and I tackled it at once. In the distance the already filling lake—among islands, but the highland still above the water, dotting it, crowned with palms and strange trees; dredgers slowly moved, native

8

canoes paddled rapidly, over all hovered great birds. To the right was the long line of the French Canal, almost submerged, stretching to the distance, against which, blue and misty and flat, were strange-shaped mountains, outlined with strange-shaped trees. Bridges like those of Hiroshigi connected island with island or with the mainland. It was perfect, the apotheosis of the Wonder of Work, and as I looked the whole rocked as with an earthquake—and then another. I was dragged into the hut as showers of stones rattled on the roof as blast after blast went off near by. Soon people in authority came up—I supposed to stop me; instead it was only to show pleasure that I found their work worth drawing. These men were all Americans, all so proud of their part in the Canal, and so strong and healthy—most of them trained and educated, I knew as soon as they opened their mouths—the greatest contrast to the crowd on the steamer, who now were all tamely following a guide and listening to what they could neither understand nor see during their only day ashore. These engineers and workmen are the sort of Americans worth knowing, and yet I did not see any golf links at Gatun. The day was spent in that telephone box and on the Spillway of the Dam —a semicircle of cyclopean concrete, backed by a bridge finer than Hokusai ever imagined, yet built to carry the huge engines that drag the long trains of dirt and rock across it, to make the dam. The dam, to me, was too big and too vague to draw. And all this is the work of my countrymen, and they are so proud of their work. Yet the men who have done this great work will tell you that we owe much to the French, and that if the engineers and the Commission at Panama had not the Government, with unlimited men and money, behind them, and the discoveries in sanitary science of which the French were ignorant, we, too, would have failed. They tell you, and show you how, the French worked on the Canal right across the Isthmus, and we are carrying out the great project they were unable to complete. And we have won the admiration of the world.

The sanitary problem is solved, but they tell you under the French, fever carried off a man for every tie that was laid on the Panama Railroad. This is a legend, but a true story is, that the French cared so little for their lives that with every shipload of

9

machinery came boxes of champagne, and those who received them asked their friends to dinner—finished the bottles—and were buried in the empty box in the morning. Now there is no fever in the Canal Zone, but there is plenty of drink in and outside of it, but, I am told, "indulged in with wonderful moderation." I certainly never saw an American under the influence of it.

In the evening a ride of two hours took me over the thirty miles to Panama—one of the last passengers over the old line of the Panama Railway, now buried under the waters of the growing lake. From the railroad I saw for the first time the primeval forest, the tropical jungle, which I had never believed in, never believed that it could not be penetrated save with an axe or a machete; but it, so, and the richness of it, the riot of it, the variety of it, is incredible and endless. The train puffed along, in that time-taking fashion of the tropics I should soon be familiar with, passing points of view I made notes of, for first impressions are for me always the best, and one trip like this gives me more ideas than days of personal pointing out. Finally Panama was reached in the dark; all I sa was a great hill lit up with rows of lights, one above the other, the night.

The day had not been hot, the sky was not blue or black—it was white, and filled with white clouds, though they were dark against it. There was no glare—and I had forgotten my sketching umbrella; but I never needed it. So far as I know, there is always a breeze—it is never really hot in the day—and as soon as the sun sets the trade wind rises—if it has not been blowing all day—and I could always sleep at night. It is all so unlike other hot countries—but, then, Panama is unlike other places: the sun rises and sets in the Pacific, and the city of Panama, though on the Pacific, is east of Colon, on the Atlantic.

There was not a smell, or a mosquito, or a fly on Ancon Hill, but over it all was the odor of petroleum, with which the streams and marshes of the whole zone are sprayed almost daily; and this has made the Canal and saved the workers.

Next morning I went to the Administration Building and presented my letters, though I did not know if I should be allowed to

10

draw. But it seemed that everything had been arranged for me by the Commission, who, it also seemed, had been doing nothing for weeks but waiting my coming. I was clothed, fed, taken about in motor cars and steam launches, given passes on the railroad, and finally turned loose to go where I wanted and draw what I liked— and if anything happened or did not happen I was just to telephone to headquarters.

The following day, donning my khaki, which I wore only once, and pocketing my pass and some oranges, I started for the locks at Pedro Miguel—pronounced, in American, Peter Megil, just as Miraflores is called Millflowers. We were all down, had breakfast, and off in the train—a jim-crow one—before the sun was up, and at Pedro Miguel station I found myself one of a horde of niggers, Greeks, Hindoos, Slovaks, Spaniards, Americans and engineers, bound for the lock, half a mile away. Here I went down to the bottom to get a drawing of the great walls that lead up to the great gates, now nearly finished. I had come at exactly the right time. These walls are surmounted with great arches and buttresses—the most dec-orative subject, the most stupendous motive I have ever seen— almost too great to draw. Unlike my experiences of a lifetime at other Government works, I was asked for no permit. I was allowed to go where I wanted, draw what I liked; when any attention was paid to me, it was to ask what I was working for—give me a glass of ice water—precious, out of the breeze at the bottom of a lock—offer to get me a photograph or make one, to suggest points of view, or tell me to clear out when a blast was to be fired. And the interest of these Americans in my work and in their work was something I had never seen before. A man in huge boots, overalls and ragged shirt, an apology for a hat, his sleeves up to his shoulders, proved himself in a minute a graduate of a great school of engineering, and proved as well his understanding of the importance of the work I was trying to do, and his regret that most painters could not see the splendid motives all about; and the greatest compliment I ever re-ceived came from one of these men, who told me my drawings " would work."

Day after day it was the same—everything, including government

11

hotels and labor trains, open to me. The only things to look out for were the blasts, the slips of dirt in the cut, and the trains, which rushed and switched about without any reference to those who might get in front of them. If one got run over, as was not usual; or blown up, which was unusual; or malaria, which few escaped among the workmen, there were plenty of hospitals, lots of nurses and sufficient doctors. Each railroad switch was attended by a little darkey with a big flag; of one of whom it was said he was seen to be asleep, with his head on the rails one day. The engineer of an approaching dirt train actually pulled up, and he was kicked awake and asked why he was taking a nap there. The boy replied he was "'termined no train go by, boss, widout me knowin' it"; and of another who, awaking suddenly and seeing half a train past his switch, pulled it open and wrecked all the trains, tracks and switches within a quarter of a mile; or the third, a Jamaican, a new hand, who, being told he was not to let a train go by, promptly signalled a locomotive to come on, and when he was hauled up, smilingly said: "Dat wan't no train wat yer tole me to stop; dat's a enjine."

Drawing had other interesting episodes connected with it, as when I sat at work in Culebra Cut the leading man of a file of niggers, carrying on his head a wooden box, would approach, stop beside me and look at the drawing. As I happened to look up I would notice the box was labelled, *Explosives, Highly dangerous.* Then, with his hands in his pockets, he and the rest of the gang would stumble along over the half-laid ties, slippery boulders and through the mud, trying to avoid the endless trains and balance the boxes on their heads at the same time. I must say, when I read the legend on the box the sensation was peculiar. They tell you, too, that when President Taft came down to the Cut all dynamiting gangs were ordered out; but one gang of blacks was forgotten, and as the train with the President and Colonel Goethals in it passed, the leader cheered so hard that he dropped his box, which somehow didn't go off. It was interesting, too, when one had been working steadily for some time, to find oneself surrounded, on getting up, by little flags, to announce that the whole place had been mined and should not be approached; or to find oneself entangled in a network of live wires ready to touch off

12

the blasts from hundreds of yards away, and to remember that I was behind a boulder about to be blown to pieces, and might be over-looked; or to be told I had better get out, as they were ready to blast, after a white man had got done chucking from one rock, to a black man on another, sticks of melanite, as the easiest way of getting them to him; or ramming in, with long poles, charges so big that trains, steam shovels and tracks had to be moved to keep them from being "shot up." I always kept out of the way as far as possible after the day at Bas Obispo when, standing some hundreds of yards from a blast watching the effect of showers of rocks falling like shells in the river, I heard wild yells, and, looking up, saw a rock as big as a foot-ball sailing toward me. I have heard one can see shells coming and dodge them. I know now that this is so, though I had to drop everything and roll to do it. But I don't like it; and accidents do happen, and there are hospitals all across the Isthmus with men, to whom accidents have happened, in them. But nothing happened to me. I did not get malaria or fever, or bitten or run over. I was very well all the time—and I walked in the sun and worked in the sun, and sat in the swamps and the bottoms of locks and at the edge of the dam, and nothing but drawings happened; but I should not advise others to try these things, nor to get too near steam shovels, which "pick up anything, from an elephant to a red-bug," but some-times drop a ton rock; nor play around near track-lifters and dirt-train emptiers—for the things are small respecters of persons. But most people do not get hurt, and I never met anyone who wanted to leave; and I believe the threat to send the men home broke the only strike on the Canal.

I did not go to Panama to study engineering—which I know nothing about; or social problems—which I had not time to master; or Central American politics—which we are in for; but to draw the Canal as it is, and the drawings are done.

I was there at the psychological moment, and am glad I went. It is not my business to answer the question: When will the Canal be opened?—though they say it will be open within a year.

Will the dam stand? Those who have built it say so.

Which is better, a sea level or a lock? The lock canal is built.

13

I did not bother myself about these things, nor about lengths and breadths and heights and depths. I went to see and draw the Canal, and during all the time I was there I was afforded every facility for seeing the construction of the Panama Canal, and from my point of view it is the most wonderful thing in the world; and I have tried to express this in my drawings at the moment before it was opened, for when it is opened, and the water turned in, half the amazing masses of masonry will be beneath the waters on one side and filled in with earth on the other, and the picturesqueness will have vanished. The Culebra Cut will be finer, and from great steamers passing through the gorge, worth going 15,000 miles, as I have done, to see. But I saw it at the right time, and have tried to show what I saw. And it is American—the work of my countrymen.

JOSEPH PENNELL

LIST OF ILLUSTRATIONS

THE ILLUSTRATIONS BEGIN WITH COLON AND PROCEED IN REGULAR SEQUENCE ACROSS THE ISTHMUS TO PANAMA.

I
COLON: THE AMERICAN QUARTER

I COLON: THE AMERICAN QUARTER

THE city of Colon is divided into two quarters—the native, or Panamanian, and the American. The former is picturesque, but has nothing to do with the Canal and is some distance from it. The Canal cannot be seen from the city. The American quarter, in which the Canal employees live, stands on the sea shore, and is made up of bungalows, shops, hotels, hospitals—all that goes to make up a city—save saloons. All are built of wood, painted white, and completely screened with wire gauze, rusted black by the dampness, a protection from mosquitoes and other beasts, bugs and vermin. Raised on concrete supports mostly with long, gently sloping roofs, and buried in a forest of palms, the town, the first the visitor will see, seems absolutely Japanese, is very pictorial and full of character. The design, I believe, of the houses was made by the American engineers or architects.

Very few of the higher Canal officers live at Colon, which is the Atlantic seaport of the Isthmus, the eastern mouth of the Canal, though Colon is west of Panama—such is the geography of the country.

The mouth of the Canal will be fortified; breakwaters and light-houses are being built.

For authorities on fortification it may be interesting to state that the forts will be so situated that the locks will be completely out of range of an enemy's guns. Personally I am not a believer in wars or navies. If my theories were practised there would be no need for fortifications.

II
MOUNT HOPE

II MOUNT HOPE

NEAR Mount Hope, which—for the French—should be
called the Slough of Despond, or the Lake of Despair,
is a huge swamp about a mile or so from Colon, on the left
bank of the French Canal, seen on the right of the lithograph. This swamp is now filled with all sorts of abandoned French machinery. Dredges, locomotives, and even
what seem to be lock gates, show amid the palms in the
distance. Huge American cranes for raising this French
material—which the American engineers have made use
of—and discharging cargo from the ships in the French
Canal—which is here finished and in use—loom over the
swamp, the banks of which are lined with piers and
workshops full of life—a curious contrast to the dead swamp
in which not a mosquito lives, nor a smell breathes.

III
GATUN: DINNER TIME

III   GATUN: DINNER TIME

BETWEEN Mount Hope and Gatun is much more of the swamp and much more abandoned machinery, but the Canal is not to be seen from the railroad, or any evidence of it, till the train stops at the station of Old Gatun, with its workmen's dwellings crowning the hillside. I regret I made no drawing of these, so picturesquely perched. At the station of Gatun—the first time I stopped—I saw the workmen—in decorative fashion—coming to the surface for dinner. The lithograph was made from a temporary bridge spanning the locks and looking toward Colon. The great machines on each side of the locks are for mixing and carrying to their place, in huge buckets, the cement and concrete, of which the locks are built. The French Canal is in the extreme distance, now used by our engineers.

IV
AT THE BOTTOM OF GATUN LOCK

IV AT THE BOTTOM OF GATUN LOCK

THERE is a flight of three double locks at Gatun by which ships will be raised eighty-five feet to the level of Gatun Lake. From the gates of the upper lock—the nearest to the Pacific—they will sail across the now-forming lake some miles (about twenty, I believe) to the Culebra Cut; through this, nine miles long, they will pass, and then descend by three other flights of locks, at Pedro Miguel and Miraflores, to the Pacific, which is twenty feet higher, I believe, than the Atlantic. The great height, eighty-five feet, was agreed upon so as to save excavation in the Cut and time in completion—one of those magnificent labor-saving devices of the moment—which I, not being an engineer, see no necessity for—having waited four hundred years for the Canal, we might, as an outsider, it seems to me, have waited four more years and got rid of a number of the locks, even if it cost more money.

The lithograph made in the middle lock shows the gates towering on either side. These gates were covered, when I made the drawing, with their armor plates. The lower parts, I was told, are to be filled with air, and the gates, worked by electricity, will virtually float. The scaffolding is only temporary, and so is the opening at the bottom and the railroad tracks, which were filled up and discarded while I was there. So huge are the locks—the three, I think, a mile long, each one thousand feet between the gates, and about ninety feet deep—that, until the men knock off, there scarce seems anyone around.

V
THE GUARD GATE, GATUN

V   THE GUARD GATE, GATUN

THERE is a safety gate in each lock, to protect, in case of accident, the main lock gate, just suggested, with the figures working at the armor-plate facing, on the extreme right.   Beyond are the outer walls and approaches of the upper lock, and beyond these, but unseen, the lake. At the bottom is the railroad and the temporary opening shown in the previous drawing.   The scale, the immensity of the whole may be judged by the size of the engines and figures.   I have never seen such a magnificent arrangement of line, light and mass, and yet those were the last things the engineers thought of.   But great work is great art, and always was and will be.   This is the Wonder of Work.

The Graving Dock

VI
APPROACHES TO GATUN LOCK

VI APPROACHES TO GATUN LOCK

THESE huge arches, only made as arches to save concrete and to break the waves of the lake, are mightier than any Roman aqueduct, and more pictorial, yet soon they will be hidden almost to the top by the waters of the lake. Electric locomotives will run out to the farthest point, and from it, tow the ships into the lock. Beyond is Gatun Lake, and to the right the lines of the French Canal and Chagres River stretch to the horizon. Even while I was on the Isthmus the river and canal disappeared forever before the waters of the rapidly rising flood. All evidence of the French work beyond Gatun has vanished under water. I did not draw the Dam or the Spillway simply because I could not find a subject to draw, or could not draw it.

VII
END OF THE DAY—GATUN LOCK

VII END OF THE DAY—GATUN LOCK

THIS was another subject I saw as the men stopped work in the evening. On the left is the stairway which most of them use, and on both sides are iron ladders which a few climb. The semicircular openings are for mooring the ships.

DANGER
KEEP OUT

VIII
THE JUNGLE
THE OLD RAILROAD FROM THE NEW

VIII   THE JUNGLE
THE OLD RAILROAD FROM THE NEW

WHILE I was on the Isthmus the old line from Gatun to the Culebra Cut at Bas Obispo was abandoned, owing to the rising waters of the lake, which will soon cover towns, and swamps, and hills, and forests. This drawing was made looking across the lake near Gatun, with the dam in the distance, and I have tried to show the rich riot of the jungle. Below, on the old road, is a steam shovel digging dirt. The little islands, charming in line, are little hills still showing above the waters of the forming lake.

IX
THE NATIVE VILLAGE

THIS lithograph was made on the new line, which dis-
covered to the visitor primitive Panama, its swamps,
jungles and native villages; but, owing to Colonel Gorgas,
native no longer, as they are odorless and clean; but the
natives, with their transformation, seem to prefer to the palm-
leaf roof, corrugated iron and tin, and abandoned freight
cars to live in.   The huts are mostly built on piles near the
rivers.   In the background can be seen the strange-shaped
mountains and strange-shaped trees.   The white tree—I
don't know its name—with the bushy top has no bark,
and is not dead, but puts out leaves, Mrs. Colonel Gaillard
tells me, in summer; and she also tells me the jungle is full
of the most wonderful orchids, birds, snakes, monkeys and
natives, and offered to take me to see them.   I saw her
splendid collection of orchids at Culebra, through the
luxuriance of which Colonel Gaillard says he has to hew his
way with a machete every morning to breakfast, so fast do
plants grow on the Isthmus.   Advantage of this rapidity of
jungle growth has been taken to bind together the completed parts of the surface of the dam, which are covered
with so much vegetation that I could not tell Nature's work
from that of the engineers.

X
THE AMERICAN VILLAGE

X THE AMERICAN VILLAGE

THESE are scattered all across the Continent, hemmed in by the tropical jungle or placed on the high, cool hill. In all there is, first, the news-stand at the station; then, the hotel—really restaurants—where on one side the Americans "gold employees" dine for thirty cents, better than they could for a dollar at home—and more decently; men, women and children. On the other, in a separate building, usually, the "silver employees" foreigners; and there are separate dining and sleeping places and cars for negroes, even on workmen's trains. The Indian has the sense and pride to live his own life down there, apart, as at home in India. There are many in the Zone.

The head men in each of these towns have their own houses; the lesser lights share double ones; and I believe the least of all, bunks; but these matters didn't interest me, nor did sanitary conditions or social evils or advantages.

There are also clubs, I believe, social centres, mothers' meetings, churches, art galleries and museums on the Isthmus, but I never saw them. I was after picturesqueness. Still, it is no wonder, under present conditions, that I never found a man who wanted to " go home "—and some hadn't been home for seven years, and dreaded going—and rightly. The Canal Zone is the best governed section of the United States.

XI
THE CUT AT BAS OBISPO

XI THE CUT AT BAS OBISPO

THE Culebra Cut commences near Bas Obispo—from this place—where the Chagres River enters Gatun Lake, the cut extends for nine miles, to Pedro Miguel. All between here and Gatun will be under water. The drawing was made at the bottom of the cut, and the various levels on which the excavations are made may be seen. The dirt trains, one above the other, are loading up from the steam shovels on each side of the old river bed in the centre. The machinery for shifting tracks and unloading trains is wonderful, but not very picturesque.

XII
IN THE CUT AT LAS CASCADAS

XII IN THE CUT AT LAS CASCADAS

THIS drawing shows the cut and gives from above some idea of the different levels on which the work is carried out. It is on some of these levels that slides have occurred and wrecked the work. The slides move slowly, not like avalanches, but have caused endless complications; but Colonel Gaillard, the engineer in charge, believes he will triumph over all his difficulties—which include even a small volcano—there is a newspaper story—but no earthquakes.

XIII
THE CUT FROM CULEBRA

XIII   THE CUT FROM CULEBRA

AT this point the cut is far the deepest at the continental divide, and here the French did their greatest work, and here this is recorded by the United States on a placque high up on the left-hand bare mountain face of Gold Hill.   The drawing was made looking towards Pedro Miguel.

XIV
STEAM SHOVEL AT WORK IN THE CULEBRA CUT

XIV STEAM SHOVEL AT WORK IN THE CULEBRA CUT

THIS beast, as they say down there, "can pick up anything from an elephant to a red-bug"—the smallest thing on the Isthmus. They also say the shovel "would look just like Teddy if it only had glasses." It does the work of digging the Canal and filling the trains, and does it amazingly—under the amazing direction of its amazing crews.

XV
THE CUT—LOOKING TOWARD CULEBRA

XV THE CUT—LOOKING TOWARD CULEBRA

THIS is the most pictorial as well as the most profound part of the cut. Culebra, the town, is high above—some of it has fallen in—on the edge in the distance—on the left. The white tower is an observatory from near which the lithograph No. XIII of the cut was made. The drawing is looking toward the Atlantic. The engineer of the dirt train—the smoke of which is so black because the engines burn oil—climbed up to see what I was at, and incidentally told me he was paid $3,600 a year, had a house free and two months' holiday. It is scarcely wonderful he has little interest in home, but the greatest pride in " our canal," and his only hope was to be " kept on the job " and run an electric locomotive for the rest of his life.

XVI
THE CUT AT PARAISO

XVI THE CUT AT PARAISO

AT THIS point the old railroad crosses the Canal bed, and there is a splended view in both directions. This is looking toward the same mountains as in the previous drawing, early in the morning. The mountains are covered with long lines of mist, under which nestles the American-Japanese town of Paraiso. The new line of railroad never crosses the Canal, but passes behind the mountain on the right. The scheme of having it follow the Canal through Culebra Cut has been abandoned, owing to the slides.

XVII
THE CUT LOOKING TOWARD ANCON HILL

XVII   THE CUT LOOKING TOWARD ANCON HILL

THIS is the view toward the Pacific from the same spot in the full stress of work.   The Pedro Miguel locks are in the distance, beyond is Ancon Hill, dominating Panama, miles farther on; and to the right, between the hills, but miles still farther, beyond Miraflores lock, the Pacific.

XVIII
LAYING THE FLOOR OF PEDRO MIGUEL LOCK

XVIII LAYING THE FLOOR OF PEDRO MIGUEL
LOCK

THIS is the most monumental piece of work on the Canal, and the most pictorial. The huge approaches, quite different in form from Gatun—for all the locks have character, and the character of their builders—are only arches to save concrete. Here were men enough laying the concrete floor—others swarming over the gates not yet covered with their armor plate. Beyond is the lock just shown between the gates.

Pennell Mitchel. Feb. 14. 1912.

XIX
THE GATES OF PEDRO MIGUEL

XIX THE GATES OF PEDRO MIGUEL

THIS is the same lock nearer the gates, and shows the great length of it from gate to gate and something of its building and construction, from my point of view.

XX
THE WALLS OF PEDRO MIGUEL

XX   THE WALLS OF PEDRO MIGUEL

THIS was drawn from the opposite end of the lock and the great side walls topped with their concrete-making crenellations and cranes are seen. In the foreground, on the left, is one of the side openings for emptying the water from one lock to another—for all the locks are double, side by side, and ships will not have to wait until a lock is empty, as is usual, before they can enter, but, as one empties, the same water partly fills the one beside it, and so steamers will pass without waiting. Two or three small vessels can go through at the same time, as well as the largest with room to spare.

XXI
BUILDING MIRAFLORES LOCK

XXI BUILDING MIRAFLORES LOCK

THIS lock, the nearest the Pacific, is again quite different and is the work of a civil engineer, Mr. Williamson, and not of army officers, like the rest. Between the two forces, I believe, the most fierce harmony exists. The drawing shows the two locks side by side, the great cranes—they are different, too—towering above. All the ground here will be filled by a small lake between this lock and Pedro Miguel.

XXII
CRANES—MIRAFLORES LOCK

XXII CRANES—MIRAFLORES LOCK

THESE great cranes travel to and fro, and as I drew the nearest I found the lines changing, but thought there was something wrong with me. So huge were they, and so silently and solemnly did they move, that I could not believe they were moving. This is the Pacific end of the lock—the last on the Canal.

XXIII
WALLS OF MIRAFLORES LOCK

XXIII   WALLS OF MIRAFLORES LOCK

THE only wall in March of the approach to Miraflores may be contrasted with the similar subject No. XX—Pedro Miguel.

Much as there was to be done in March, the engineer, Mr. Williamson, had no doubt it would be finished this fall; for as fast as the other locks were completed, men and machines were to be put on this.

XXIV
OFFICIAL ANCON

XXIV OFFICIAL ANCON

AMID these royal palm groves work and live many of the members of the Isthmian Canal Commission—the rest are on the high hill at Culebra.   To the secretary, Mr. J. B. Bishop, and to his family, I am endlessly indebted for endless help while on the Zone.

Ancon is a perfect Japanese town—built by Americans —and the interiors of the houses here and at Culebra are as delightful as their owners are charming—and I know of what I speak.   The large building against the ocean is the Administration Office of the Isthmian Canal Commission.

XXV
FROM ANCON HILL

XXV FROM ANCON HILL

A ROAD winds up Ancon Hill, passing the official residences and the hospitals, finally reaching a terrace bordered with royal palms. Below to the left is the Tivoli Hotel, and still lower and farther away, the city, while the Pacific fills the distance. This is the most beautiful spot I saw on the Isthmus.

XXVI
THE CATHEDRAL, PANAMA

XXVI THE CATHEDRAL, PANAMA

THE Cathedral, one of a number of churches in the city of Panama, stands in a large square. The feeling of all these, with their richly decorated façades and long, unbroken side walls, is absolutely Spanish—but the interiors are far more bare—much more like Italian churches.

XXVII

THE CITY OF PANAMA
FROM THE TIVOLI HOTEL, ANCON

XXVII THE CITY OF PANAMA
FROM THE TIVOLI HOTEL, ANCON

FROM the wing of the Government hotel in which I
stayed I looked out over the city of Panama to the Pacific.
If this city were in Spain, or if even a decent description
of it were in a European guide-book, the hordes of Americans who go to the Canal would rave over it. As it is, not
many of them (not being told) ever see it, though there
are few towns in Europe with more character. But I
regret to say my countrymen don't know what they are
looking at, or what to look at, till they have a guide-book,
courier or tout to tell them. The Government provides,
I am told, a Harvard graduate to perform the latter
function, and sends out daily an observation car across the
Continent.

The two strange, flat-topped mountains, miles out at sea,
are to be fortified, and they are so far from shore, and
the locks so far inland, as to be out of range—as well as out
of sight—of modern guns and gunners.

XXVIII
THE MOUTH OF THE CANAL FROM THE SEA

XXVIII   THE MOUTH OF THE CANAL FROM THE
SEA

THIS drawing was made from the channel which leads out to the Pacific Ocean. The mouth of the Canal is on the left in the flat space between the mountains; on the right of this, the dark mass on the edge of the water is the docks and harbors; then comes the great, towering Ancon Hill, one side all dug out in terraces for dirt, much of which goes to fill in the outside of locks, which, however, will work before they are filled in. And for what other purposes the War Department are going to use this Gibraltar they alone know. The other side, a mass of palms shelters the houses of the officials, and at the foot of the hill, to the right, Panama—as beautiful as Naples or Tangier, yet hardly a tourist knows it; and—well, the Government is not running a tourist agency.

The breakwater, which will connect the fortified islands miles away with the mainland, is just started in the centre. This is the first and last view of Panama—and of the greatest work of modern times, the work of the greatest engineers of all time.   JOSEPH PENNELL